STONE AGE FARMERS BESIDE THE SEA

Scotland's Prehistoric Village of Skara Brae

by **Caroline Arnold**
Photographs by **Arthur P. Arnold**

CLARION BOOKS/*New York*

With thanks to Cynthia Watters, Bill Grisham,
and Anne-Marie Schaaf for encouraging us to visit
the Orkneys and to David Lea for his enthusiastic and
informative tour of the islands.
—C. A. and A. A.

Title page: *View of Skaill House from Skara Brae*
Page 2-3: *The Old Man of Hoy (on the Orkney coast).*

Clarion Books
a Houghton Mifflin Company imprint
215 Park Avenue South, New York, NY 10003
Text copyright © 1997 by Caroline Arnold
Photographs copyright © 1997 by Arthur P. Arnold

Type is 12/17-point Kuenstler

For information about this and other Houghton Mifflin trade and reference
books and multimedia products, visit The Bookstore at Houghton Mifflin
on the World Wide Web at (http://www.hmco.com/trade/).

Printed in China

Library of Congress Cataloging-in-Publication Data
Arnold, Caroline.
    Stone Age farmers beside the sea : Scotland's prehistoric village of Skara Brae / by
Caroline Arnold ; photographs by Arthur P. Arnold.
        p   cm.
    Includes index.
    Summary: Describes the Stone Age settlement preserved in the sand dunes on one of
Scotland's Orkney Islands, telling how it was discovered and what it reveals about life in
prehistoric times.
    ISBN 0-395-77601-5
    1. Skara Brae Site (Scotland)—Juvenile literature.   2. Neolithic period—Scotland—
Juvenile literature.   3. Scotland—Antiquities—Juvenile literature [1. Skara Brae Site
Scotland) 2. Scotland—Antiquities. 3. Man, Prehistoric.]   I. Title.
GN776.22.G7A77   1997
936.1'132—dc20   96-20021
                                        CIP
                                        AC

TPN 10 9 8 7 6 5 4 3 2 1

CONTENTS

A wide embankment surrounding Skara Brae provides views into the ancient dwellings.

VILLAGE BY THE SEA

On a windswept island at the northern tip of Scotland, thick stone walls lie half buried by the edge of the sea. They are the remains of Skara Brae (pronounced Scar-a Bray), one of Europe's oldest known and best preserved prehistoric villages. Five thousand years ago ancient farmers tended livestock and tilled the earth on land surrounding the village. They also hunted wildlife and fished along the coast. Their houses, built of sturdy stone, were clustered in a compact unit and joined along an inner passageway. They were the heart of a close-knit agricultural community and may have been home to as many as twenty families at one time.

People lived at Skara Brae for about six hundred years, from 3100 to 2500 B.C. After they left, wind blew sand from the surrounding dunes over the village and buried it. For thousands of years Skara Brae was forgotten. It was not until its discovery almost 150 years ago that the life of its inhabitants became known once again.

Today visitors to Skara Brae can explore the remains of the village and see many of the ancient objects found during its excavation. No other place in northern Europe provides such a complete picture of life in the Neolithic, or New Stone Age, a period of human history when people made tools with stone or bone and began to live in settled communities.

5

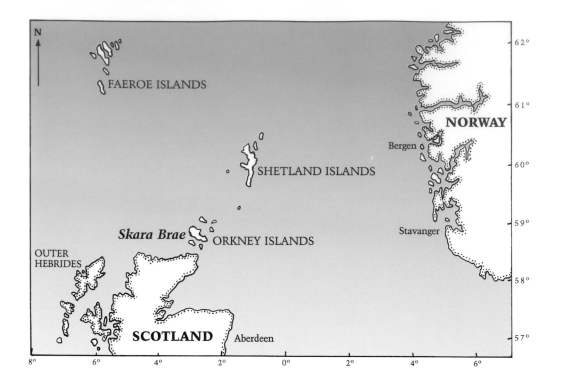

THE ORKNEY LANDSCAPE

Skara Brae is in the Orkneys, a group of more than seventy islands at the northern tip of Scotland. The islands have been continuously inhabited for more than five thousand years, and the landscape, which is dotted with the remains of ancient dwellings, tombs, and other structures from the past, is an archeologist's paradise. Prehistoric sites in the Orkneys range from the giant standing stones of Neolithic times to the ruins of Viking settlements built in the eleventh century A.D.

The village of Skara Brae was built near the shore of a bay on the west side of one of the largest Orkney islands called Mainland. Five thousand years ago the shoreline was more distant and separated from the houses by sand. Wind and erosion have destroyed the dunes, increasing the size of the bay, so its shore is now nearly at the edge of the village. The name Skara Brae comes from Scottish words meaning *hilly dunes*.

(ABOVE) *The ruins of Skara Brae face the Bay of Skaill.*

(BELOW) *The standing stones of the Ring of Brodgar were erected during the same period that people were living at Skara Brae.*

The weather in the Orkneys is often wet and windy, and in the winter of 1850, a series of violent storms battered the islands, pounding them with fierce waves and gale force winds. One of these storms was so severe that it blew away the grass and sand from a high dune on land owned by William Watt, the Laird of Skaill. (*Laird* is the Scottish word for *lord*, a British hereditary title.) When the storm subsided, William Watt went out to inspect the damage to his property. As he crossed the land that separated his fields from the sea, he saw that the wind and waves had exposed the remains of an ancient village, which had been buried beneath the sand. For the first time in more than forty centuries, the dwellings of Skara Brae were exposed to the open air. As William Watt uncovered the ruins he discovered more stone walls, furniture, stone and bone tools, pottery, beads, and other objects. The sand and surrounding embankment had protected the houses and the items in them so well that many were in almost perfect condition.

Between 1850 and 1868 William Watt excavated four of the houses at Skara Brae and collected a large number of stone tools and other objects that are now in the collection of the British Museum. Even though he was not a trained archeologist, William Watt knew that the ruins on his property were unusual and provided important clues to how some of the earliest inhabitants of the islands once lived.

The manor house of the Laird of Skaill stands about a quarter of a mile from the ruins of Skara Brae.

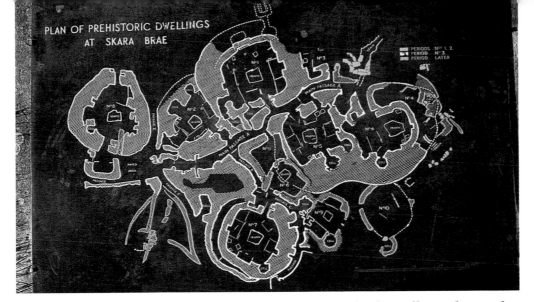

A diagram of the Skara Brae ruins shows the thick walls and circular design of the buildings.

After William Watt died, the government of Great Britain became the guardian of the ruins at Skara Brae. Because the village was so close to the water, one of its first projects was the building of a seawall to prevent possible future damage from big storms. The first professional excavations at Skara Brae were conducted between 1928 and 1930 under the supervision of Professor Gordon Childe, an expert in British prehistory. That work revealed several more houses in addition to those William Watt had excavated, as well as the foundations of an earlier village underneath them.

Skara Brae was built twice during the six centuries of its occupation. Most of the structures on view today are from the second stage of construction. Only a few of the earlier houses, those that were not covered by later structures, have been exposed.

A third excavation of Skara Brae was conducted in 1972 and 1973. New methods of scientific analysis, not yet available at the time of the earlier work at Skara Brae, confirmed the ancient origins of the village and established more precisely the dates of many of the objects found there.

(LEFT) *Walkways allow visitors to look into buildings.*

Like most of the people who live in the Orkneys today, the early set-tlers were farmers and fishermen who relied on the land and the sea to provide them with the things they needed to live.

THE FIRST SETTLERS

Farming as a way of life began about twelve thousand years ago when people living in the Middle East began to grow some of their own food. Over the next six thousand years the practice spread throughout Europe. Farming made it possible for people to produce more food. It also meant that they could stay in the same place year round, so for the first time people began to live in permanent settlements. It is known that people were farming in parts of Scotland as early as 4000 B.C.

The first settlers in the Orkneys arrived about 3700 B.C. and came from farming communities in northern Scotland. They crossed the water in boats made of animal skins and pulled their supplies behind them on wooden rafts. They brought with them seeds for planting, as well as cattle, sheep, and pigs for livestock.

When people first came to the Orkneys, the islands looked much the same as they do today—a combination of rocky coastline and a rolling, nearly treeless landscape. Although the Orkneys are located as far north as Hudson Bay in Canada, warm ocean currents result in a moderate climate suitable for growing crops. The earliest settlements in the Orkneys were family farms consisting of one or two houses and a few small sheds surrounded by fields and pastures. The Knap of Howar on the island of Papa Westray is the oldest known farm of this type in the Orkneys. Archeologists believe people were living there between about 3700 and 2800 B.C.

People began to live at Skara Brae around 3100 B.C. Skara Brae was unusual because it was a village of several families rather than a single family farm. It represents a change from living independently on scattered farms to life together in organized communities. The ruins of three other villages similar to Skara Brae have been found in the Orkneys. They are located at Rinyo, Noltland, and Pierowell, and archeologists believe that there may be several other sites as well.

BUILDING SKARA BRAE

From ancient times to the present, the primary building material in the Orkneys has been stone. There is an abundant local supply, and the slabs can be easily cut into large flat pieces suitable for building. One of the reasons we know so much about neolithic life at Skara Brae is that stone is extremely durable and changes little over time.

Archeologists believe that another important construction material for the ancient inhabitants of the Orkneys was whalebone. Although the early settlers probably did not have large boats or powerful enough weapons to hunt whales at sea, they could have obtained bone from whales that washed up onto the shore. Whales may have also provided meat, oil, and materials for making tools.

Wood has always been scarce in the Orkneys. The few species of trees native to the islands are too small to provide timber. In ancient times the main source of wood for building came from large trees that washed up on the beach as driftwood. These trees had grown far away in the forests of North America. They had then fallen into rivers and were washed out to sea, where strong ocean currents carried them across the Atlantic. (Many centuries later these same currents brought Viking explorers home from their explorations of North America.)

(ABOVE) *Orkney sandstone breaks naturally into slabs.*

(BELOW LEFT) *In some houses at Skara Brae, the stone walls are nearly ten feet high.* (BELOW RIGHT) *The construction of stone walls in the Orkneys has changed little over time.*

All of the houses at Skara Brae are about the same size and have an average floor space of about 387 square feet each.

The basic design of each house at Skara Brae is the same—a square room with rounded corners plus several small alcoves for storing food or fuel. Cavities or nooks in the walls provided additional storage areas. Drains in the floor of some of the alcoves suggest that they may have been used as bathrooms.

The first houses built at Skara Brae were free-standing, with little outside support. Houses built during the second stage of construction had walls held up on one side by a thick, earthen mound. The mound was made of *midden*—trash mixed with soil and plant matter. Villagers built up the midden over a long period of time by piling together plants, ash, shells, broken bones, animal dung, stone, pottery, and other waste from their everyday activities. Just as in a modern compost pile, the plants decayed over time, turning into small, moist particles. When mixed with the other materials, they formed a hard, clay-like substance. Today the "trash" embedded in the midden provides archeologists with valuable information about the daily life of the people of Skara Brae.

When villagers began to build a house, they heaped the midden into a large mound and dug into the center to make a space for building. Walls for houses and passageways were constructed by piling flat stones in layers. No cement held the stones together, but the solid bank of midden on the outside helped support them. The midden also prevented moisture and cold air from seeping through the cracks between the stones and made the stone walls weatherproof.

The village of Skara Brae is a cluster of one-room houses joined by covered passages. Today these buildings are open to the sky, but in ancient times they would have been covered by low roofs. Although stones now cover a few of the narrower passages, experts believe that stone was not used as roofing material for the houses. Rather, they believe, the houses had rafters made of whalebone or wood that were then covered with sod and held down by ropes. (Fragments of rope made from twisted heather have been found in the midden.)

The covered passageways that linked the houses at Skara Brae allowed people to visit each other without going outside. Doorways placed along a common inside passageway, instead of facing directly outdoors, protected inhabitants from cold drafts. Doors were made either of wood or stone, and a whalebone or wooden bar held each door in place.

Passageways between houses were once covered with large stone slabs.

This freestanding structure is believed to have been used as a workshop. Its walls are more than 6.5 feet thick.

THE WORKSHOP

Most of the structures visible at Skara Brae today are dwellings where people once lived. One building, however, separated from the houses and without support from midden, is believed to be a workshop. Although it has a central hearth, it has no beds or dresser, so it does not appear that people lived there. When the building was excavated, stone fragments found on the floor suggested that this place may have been used for making tools and hunting weapons.

Although sandstone for building was abundant in the Orkneys, harder stones like flint or chert, which were needed to make tools, were not readily available. Flint can be flaked to make a sharp edge for a knife, but its only source in the Orkneys was from pebbles washed onto the shore from deposits deep in the ocean. Chert could be found at two sites, but the pieces were small and not easily shaped into sharp tools. So unlike neolithic communities in most other places, the people in the Orkneys made many of their tools from bone or wood.

Hundreds of tools have been found at Skara Brae. They include axes for chopping, mattocks for hoeing, knives for cutting, and scrapers for cleaning skins. A number of beautifully carved objects that may have had ceremonial purposes have also been found.

(LEFT) *Casts of stone tools found at Skara Brae.*
(RIGHT) *Bone tools and necklace.*

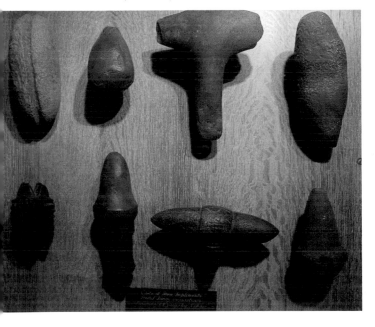

large bone borers

DAILY LIFE IN NEOLITHIC TIMES

The focus of each dwelling at Skara Brae, as in other neolithic homes, was a stone-bordered hearth. The hearth fire was both a source of light and heat as well as a place for cooking food. Fuel for burning probably came from animal dung, dried seaweed, heather and bracken, and from whalebone, rich in oil. The little wood available to the inhabitants of Skara Brae was not burned because it was needed for building and for making handles for tools.

The atmosphere inside the houses at Skara Brae was probably rather dark and smoky. Houses had no windows and no chimneys. Smoke from the fire could escape only through holes in the roof.

The furniture of Skara Brae was mostly made of stone. In some houses you can see stone seats or benches beside the hearth. The largest seat always faced the doorway and may have been where the head of household sat.

Along the walls of many houses you can see box beds where people once slept. The large stone slabs facing the fire would have absorbed the heat and helped make the bed warm. Although these beds do not look particularly comfortable now, in ancient times they were probably filled with bracken or other plants to make springy mattresses. Tall posts at the corners of the beds may have supported shelves over the beds or canopies made of skins. These would have kept in heat and protected the sleeper from getting wet if the roof leaked. Animal skins would have been used as blankets.

(ABOVE) *Large stone slabs enclosed box beds.*

(BELOW) *Heather may have been used to make soft mattresses.*

The largest piece of furniture in each house at Skara Brae was the stone dresser, or shelf, that stood against the wall opposite the doorway. It was a place where food and other belongings could be stored and where a family may have displayed its most prized belongings.

Pottery made from locally found clay was used for cooking and storage. Archeologists classify the pottery from Skara Brae as "grooved ware." This same kind of flat-bottomed pottery is found on the south coast of England and links the Orkneys with neolithic traditions elsewhere in Britain.

This reconstruction of a neolithic dresser is located in the town of Kirkwall at the Tankerness Museum, where many neolithic artifacts are on display.

25

Small water tanks set in the floor in front of the dresser may have held fish bait or a supply of fresh water.

A common feature of the houses at Skara Brae are the shallow stone boxes built into the floor. In ancient times the corners of these boxes were sealed with clay to make them watertight. The boxes may simply have been places to store fresh water. Many experts think, however, that these tanks were used to soak small shellfish called limpets. After soaking for several days the limpets became soft and could be used either as food or fish bait.

Most fishing by the people of Skara Brae was probably done in shallow water along the coast, either from small boats or from the shore. Seafood remains found in the midden indicate that villagers ate cod and other fish as well as lobster, crab, mussels, sea urchins, and oysters. Bones of whales and seals reveal that these sea animals were sources of food as well.

When archeologists excavated Skara Brae they also found an enormous number of animal bones, an indication that meat was an important part of the neolithic diet. People ate several kinds of meat including beef, lamb, pork, goat, and venison. Cattle, sheep, and goats provided milk to drink. Broken eggshells in the midden suggest that people also collected the eggs of wild birds for food.

Deer were brought to the Orkneys from Scotland by some of the first settlers. The animals, which were allowed to roam wild, quickly adapted to their new habitat and provided a source of large game for the settlers to hunt.

We know less about the kinds of plant foods the people of Skara Brae ate, as plant materials do not preserve the way shells and bones do. It is likely that people collected wild nuts and berries in addition to growing some of their own food. Experts believe that crops were fertilized with material from the village midden and with seaweed.

To prepare the soil for planting seeds, neolithic farmers used a pointed tool called an ard to scratch furrows into the ground. Some of these ancient plow marks are still visible in an ancient Orkney field excavated near the village of Noltland.

Although the climate in the Orkneys today is too cold for growing wheat or barley as commercial crops, the average temperature in neolithic times was slightly warmer. Samples of wheat and barley have been found at Skara Brae, and in several houses are stone slabs, called querns, where the grain was ground into meal. The meal may have been used to make bread or a kind of porridge.

Wild nuts and berries supplemented homegrown food in the diet.

(ABOVE) *Barley was an important food crop in ancient times.*

(RIGHT) *Handheld grinding stones crushed grain on the stone below.*

Although neolithic sheep were less woolly than modern breeds, their skins would have made warm cloaks.

The sheep that people kept in ancient times were different from their modern descendants in that they did not produce thick wool. So although the sheep at Skara Brae would have provided meat and skins, their wool was not suitable for weaving into fabric.

We do not know what the villagers of Skara Brae wore, but experts think that clothing was made mostly of leather or fur. Numerous tools for preparing and sewing leather have been excavated. The skins for making clothing probably came either from domestic animals or from wild animals, such as deer or sea otters. People may have added the soft feathers of ducks and other wild seabirds to their clothes to give them extra warmth.

The people of Skara Brae also wore jewelry. When archeologists were excavating an alcove in one of the houses at Skara Brae, they found a container with 2400 beads, pendants, and pins inside. The beads may have been strung on necklaces or perhaps sewn onto clothing. Most of these decorative items are bone, but a few are made of stone or wood. The archeologists also found a small whalebone dish containing a red pigment. This may have been used as a paint or stain for body decoration or for adding color to carvings or other household objects.

Bones from seabirds like these gannets were used to make awls and other tools for working leather.

LIFE AND DEATH

One of the ways that archeologists learn how people lived in ancient times is to study the way they treated their dead. More than seventy tombs from the Neolithic period have been discovered in the Orkneys. These ancient burial places contain both human and animal bones as well as stone tools, pottery, and other household objects. The wealth of material found at the sites provides information about the physical characteristics of the people who were buried there and about the objects they valued.

Neolithic tombs in the Orkneys range from simple structures to large, sophisticated monuments. Archeologists believe that the smaller tombs marked the territories of local clans. A clan would have used its tomb both to house the remains of its dead and also as a place to perform ceremonial rites. Larger tombs, such as that at Maes Howe, were built for more important regional clan chiefs. This stone chamber, built in the shape of a cross, is nearly 18 feet high in the center. After the tomb was finished, a ditch was dug around it and the outside was completely covered with dirt except for a narrow entrance passage. At midwinter, the setting sun shines through this passage and lights the interior of the tomb. Because of the size and fine workmanship of Maes Howe, experts think that it may have been built for a clan chief who ruled over the whole area.

When the tomb at Maes Howe is viewed from a distance, it looks like a small hill rising above the adjacent fields.

33

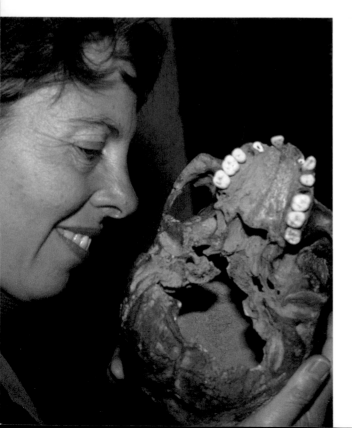

(ABOVE) *Vertical stones divide the Tomb of the Eagles into chambers. Bones were deposited in piles inside alcoves along the floor.*

(LEFT) *Ancient skulls provide information about an individual's health and physical traits.*

One of the most interesting smaller burial sites in the Orkneys is the tomb at Isbister. This structure was discovered by accident in 1958 by a farmer digging in one of his fields. Because the tomb contained an unusual number of sea eagle bones it is also known as the Tomb of the Eagles. The eagle may have been a totem, or symbol, of the clan that built the tomb. Several other tombs in the Orkneys also contain unusual animal bones—dogs at two tombs, songbirds at one, and cormorants at another—suggesting that each clan may have had its own animal totem.

The Tomb of the Eagles was first constructed about 3300 B.C. and was used for about eight hundred years. When it was excavated, more than sixteen thousand human bones, representing the remains of 342 individuals, were found in it. Measurements taken from these bones show that the average adult male in Neolithic Orkney was about 5 feet 7 inches tall and the average woman was 5 feet 3.5 inches tall. Most people were strong and muscular, which is not surprising since they lived an active, outdoor life. Many skeletons have an unusual alteration in the ankle bones that experts think may have developed from climbing cliffs to get eggs or birds. The bones also indicate that many people in ancient Orkney suffered from arthritis.

Many of the women's skulls from the Tomb of the Eagles have depressions across the forehead. This suggests that women carried loads or babies on their backs and used a band around the head for support. Teeth in the skulls have no cavities, but they do show signs of wear from chewing grit that became mixed with grain during the grinding process.

Life must have been difficult five thousand years ago in the Orkneys. Many people died as young children and for those who survived childhood, the average age of death was between the ages of fifteen and thirty. The few individuals who survived to fifty would have been considered extremely old.

GIANT STANDING STONES

Among the most fascinating and mystical ruins of Neolithic times in Britain are huge circular ditches and banks called henges. Some henge monuments, like Stonehenge in England, had rings of standing stones or wooden posts within the earthen circle. Others had no large structures.

Just six miles from Skara Brae, you can see two henge monuments, the Ring of Brodgar and the Stones of Stennis. Both of these henges have standing stones and are part of the greater ceremonial area that lies between the Loch of Harray and the Loch of Stennis. (*Loch* is the Scottish word for *lake*.) These two henge monuments, as well as other standing stones and burial mounds, mark this area as a sacred place. It must have taken enormous effort to create these giant circles, which suggests that they had special, important purposes. In ancient times, people from all over the Orkneys, including the residents of Skara Brae, gathered at these henges for ceremonial activities. Although much speculation exists about the exact meaning of the henges, the details of what went on in these places is not known.

The circle of the Stones of Stennis is the earliest of the two Orkney henges. In the center you can see four stone slabs bordering an area that resembles a large hearth. In ancient times a small wooden structure and a single tall wooden post stood in the circle. The post may have been a kind of marker that made the ring into a giant sundial. The standing stones once formed part of a circle that measured nearly one hundred feet across. Of the original twelve Stones of Stennis, only three remain standing.

Sheep now graze among the Stones of Stennis.

The Ring of Brodgar is one of the largest henges in Britain. The ditch around it was originally eleven feet deep and thirty-three feet across at the top, and the total work time of the people who built it is estimated to have been 80,000 hours. The interior of the ring is 338 feet across and originally had a circle of sixty stones. These huge slabs were cut from a quarry to the north of Skara Brae.

Some experts think that standing stones, like those in the Orkneys, were erected as part of a network to make observations on the solar system. Sight lines connecting the Ring of Brodgar and nearby burial mounds with prominent landmarks may have been used to predict cycles of the moon in ancient times.

Heather lines the ditch around the standing stones of the Ring of Brodgar.

THE END OF SKARA BRAE

The village of Skara Brae was abandoned about 4500 years ago and never lived in again. Some experts think that the inhabitants of Skara Brae were forced to leave their village suddenly when it was destroyed by a violent storm such as the one that uncovered it in 1850. Other experts think, however, that people left the village gradually, one family at a time, until no one remained. Wind from the sea slowly blew sand over the houses until they were buried and finally forgotten. In either case, village life all over the Orkneys declined at this period in history, possibly because regional activities at places like the Ring of Brodgar and Maes Howe became more important as a focus of people's lives. They no longer needed the kind of neighborly support that village life provided.

As the houses of Skara Brae were abandoned, the roofs collapsed and the rooms filled with sand.

Cooking troughs like this one at Liddle Burnt Mount were widely used in the Orkneys about 1000 B.C.

Over time people in the Orkneys gradually developed new customs and learned new ways to do things. The Neolithic Age was followed by the Bronze Age, a time when people began to make tools and ornaments from bronze. (Bronze is a metal made by combining copper and tin.) Although many examples of beautiful jewelry and bronze-bladed knives from this period have been found elsewhere in northern Europe, bronze items are rare in the Orkneys. With no local sources, bronze had to be imported. The Bronze Age lasted from about 2000 to about 600 B.C.

The quality of life in the Orkneys declined in the later Bronze Age. The climate became colder and wetter and made farming more difficult. Huge marshy areas turned into peat, a material that can be burned for fuel. Among the archeological remains from this period are large heaps of stones found next to deep water tanks set into the ground. Experts think that people heated the stones in peat fires and then plunged them into the water to make it boil for cooking.

In the Iron Age, people started to make tools of iron, a metal that was easier to find and more durable than bronze. During this period people in northern Britain were building tall defensive towers called brochs. The ruins of some of these structures can be seen at several places in the Orkneys, usually on high points of land jutting out toward the sea.

The prehistory period of Orkney history ends with the Viking, or Norse, occupation. Norse earls ruled the Orkneys from about 800 A.D. until the Orkneys became part of Scotland in 1468. The Orkneys are located less than three hundred miles from the Norwegian coast, and the Norse influence can still be seen in some of the building and place names on the islands. For instance, St. Magnus Cathedral, in the town of Kirkwall, was built in 1137 in honor of Magnus Erlendson, a Norse earl who ruled over Orkney in the eleventh century.

(LEFT) *The Broch of Gurness was first built about 500 B.C.*
(RIGHT) *St. Magnus Cathedral.*

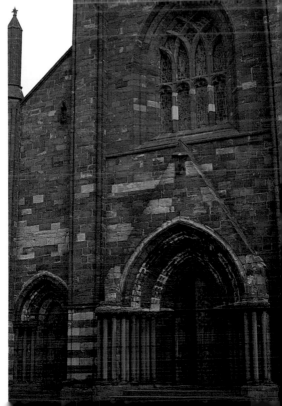

Of all the ancient sites in the Orkneys, Skara Brae is among the most remarkable. As you peer over the village walls today it is not hard to imagine families sitting around their hearths long ago, talking and eating while children played and neighbors came to visit. With firelight dancing across the walls and winter winds roaring outside, these sturdy stone houses would have been a welcome retreat from the weather, a place where people could feel safe and secure.

Skara Brae is amazing both because it is so old and because so much has been preserved. People were living at Skara Brae before the Egyptians built their pyramids, before ancient Americans built their first cities, and before the Chinese built the Great Wall. Skara Brae is a window onto some of our most ancient history. For those of us with roots in northern Europe, the ruins at Skara Brae provide fascinating clues to how some of our most remote ancestors actually lived.

The stones of Skara Brae tell the story of one of Europe's earliest farming communities.

GLOSSARY

archeologists—people who dig up, identify, and sometimes remove evidence of earlier cultures.

archeology—the study of a prehistoric culture by excavation and description of its remains.

ard—a pointed tool used for scratching furrows into the ground for planting.

artifact—humanmade object or change to the environment made by humans.

bracken—large, coarse ferns.

Broch of Gurness—ruins of an Iron Age tower in the Orkney Islands; it was built around 500 B.C.

brochs—tall, defensive stone towers built in the north and west of Scotland and nearby islands during the Iron Age.

Bronze Age—in Europe from about 3000 to 1000 B.C.; in the Orkneys from 2000 to 600 B.C.; a period when people began to make tools and ornaments from bronze.

chert—a type of quartz that can be shaped into tools; similar to flint but not as easily worked.

clan—a tribe of people descended from a common ancestor and united under a chieftain.

dung—animal manure; when dried it can be used as fuel.

flint—a type of very hard quartz that can be flaked to form a sharp-edged stone tool.

gannets—large seabirds in the pelican family; they typically nest in large colonies on sea cliffs.

grooved ware—a type of flat-bottomed pottery found at a number of neolithic sites in Britain.

heather—a low-growing plant of the heath family; it has stalks of purplish-pink flowers.

henge—a circular ditch and bank often enclosing standing stones or other structures; known only in Britain.

Iron Age—from about 1000 B.C. to 100 A.D.; some authorities extend this period to modern times.

Knap of Howar—oldest known settlement in the Orkney Islands; it was occupied between 3700 and 2800 B.C.

limpet—a small shellfish with an open conical shell; usually found clinging to rocks in shallow water.

Maes Howe—a large neolithic tomb in the Orkneys; considered to be the supreme example of neolithic architecture in northern Europe.

mattock—a tool for loosening the soil or digging up and cutting roots; like a pickax but with a flat blade on both ends.

midden—a material made by mixing trash with earth and plant matter.

Neolithic Age (also called the **New Stone Age**)—about 9000 to about 3000 B.C. or later; a period of history when people made tools from stone and bone and began to domesticate plants and animals.

peat—a turf cut from swampland and dried and used as fuel or fertilizer.

prehistory—events that occurred before recorded history.

quern—a handmill for grinding grain; consists of two stone disks, one upon the other.

Ring of Brodgar—neolithic henge monument in the Orkney Islands.

Skara Brae—neolithic village in the Orkney Islands; occupied between 3100 and 2500 B.C.

standing stones—enormous stone posts erected in neolithic times at henges and other sacred places in Britain.

Stonehenge—ditch and standing stones in southern England, near Salisbury.

Stones of Stennis—neolithic henge monument in the Orkney Islands.

Tomb of the Eagles (also called **Isbister Tomb**)—a cliff-top neolithic tomb in the Orkney Islands; used from 3300 to 2500 B.C.

totem—an animal or natural object taken as the emblem or symbol of a family, clan, or group.

venison—the meat of deer.

Vikings (also called **Norsemen**)—Scandinavian raiders, traders, and colonists who roamed Europe and neighboring lands between 800 and 1000 A.D.; discovered North America about 1000 A.D.; occupied the Orkneys until 1468.

Photo credit: Anne–Marie Schaaf, p. 26; Caroline Arnold, p. 23 bottom.

Rocky stack on the Orkney coast.

INDEX